D0384913

risotto

simple and delicious step-by-step recipes

Bernice Hurst

p

This is a Parragon Publishing Book
First published in 2002

Parragon Publishing
Queen Street House
4 Queen Street
Bath, BA1 1HE, UK

Copyright © Parragon 2002

All rights reserved. No part of this publication
may be reproduced, stored in a retrieval system, or
transmitted, in any form or by any means, electronic,
mechanical, photocopying, recording, or otherwise,
without the prior permission of the copyright holder.

ISBN: 0-75258-897-4

Printed in China

Produced by the Bridgewater Book Company Ltd.

Photographer Ian Parsons

Home Economist Sara Hesketh

NOTES FOR THE READER

- This book uses both imperial and metric measurements. Follow the same units of measurement throughout; do not mix imperial and metric.

- All spoon measurements are level: teaspoons are assumed to be 5 ml, and tablespoons are assumed to be 15 ml.

- Unless otherwise stated, milk is assumed to be whole milk, eggs and individual vegetables such as carrots are medium, and pepper is freshly ground black pepper.

- Recipes using raw eggs should be avoided by infants, the elderly, pregnant women, convalescents, and anyone suffering from an illness.

- The times given are an approximate guide only. Preparation times differ according to the techniques used by different people and the cooking times may also vary from those given. Optional ingredients, variations, or serving suggestions have not been included in the calculations.

contents

introduction

Once the basic method for cooking risotto has been mastered, flavorings and accompaniments are entirely a matter of taste, mood, and availability. Extra ingredients can be added at the very beginning of the cooking process, along with an onion or shallot. Or they can be cooked separately and gently folded in just a few minutes before the risotto has finished cooking so that flavors can blend. Or they can be cooked separately and served as a garnish to the finished dish.

The best rice for risotto is super-fino, generally available as arborio, carnaroli, roma, or vialone nano. The grains are long and absorbent with a high level of starch. When cooked slowly, with only gradual additions of liquid, the grains become plump and soft on the outside while retaining some bite at the center. It is a relatively long and slow process, normally needing a good 20 minutes' cooking time, with constant attention and stirring to prevent the rice sticking, but it is well worth the effort.

Risotto is delicious and filling. As with most cookery books, this one has a selection of recipes that should not only make delicious dining but, hopefully, provide inspiration and set you off on the path to create your own recipes.

guide to recipe key		
	easy	Recipes are graded as follows: 1 pea = easy; 2 peas = very easy; 3 peas = extremely easy.
	serves 4	Recipes generally serve four people. Simply halve the ingredients to serve two, taking care not to mix imperial and metric measurements.
	15 minutes	Preparation time. Where marinating or chilling are involved, these times have been added on separately: eg, 15 minutes + 30 minutes to marinate.
	25 minutes	Cooking time.

basic basil risotto
page 48

risotto with tuna & pine nuts
page 56

shredded spinach and ham risotto
page 66

lemon & veal risotto
page 88

vegetarian

The key to a successful risotto is its consistency—slightly loose, creamy, and smooth with just the smallest bite left in the rice. Most creamy Italian cheeses that melt well can be substituted for all or part of the Parmesan when making risotto, whether it's Basic Risotto, Wild Mushroom Risotto, or Double Tomato Risotto. Try using Fontina, Taleggio, or Gorgonzola to ring the changes. Experiment with flavors for the cheese and other ingredients to see which combinations suit your taste best of all.

basic risotto

		ingredients	
	extremely easy	8 cups bouillon or water	2¼ cups arborio rice
		1 tbsp olive oil	1 cup freshly grated Parmesan
	serves 4	3 tbsp butter	or Grana Padano
		1 small onion, chopped finely	salt and pepper
	5 minutes		
	20 minutes		

Bring the bouillon to a boil, then reduce the heat and keep simmering gently on a low heat while you are cooking the risotto. Heat the oil with 2 tablespoons of butter in a deep pan over a medium heat until the butter has melted. Stir in the onion and cook gently until soft and starting to turn golden. Do not brown.

Add the rice and mix to coat in oil and butter. Cook and stir for 2–3 minutes, or until the grains are translucent. Gradually add the bouillon, a ladle at a time. Stir constantly and add more liquid as the rice absorbs it. Increase the heat to moderate so that the liquid bubbles. Cook for 20 minutes, or until all the liquid is absorbed. Season to taste, but don't add too much salt as the Parmesan cheese is salty. The finished risotto should be of a creamy consistency with a bit of bite in the rice.

Remove the risotto from the heat and add the remaining butter. Mix well, then stir in the Parmesan until it melts. Season and serve.

wild mushroom risotto

		ingredients	
extremely easy		1 quantity basic risotto (see page 8) made with vegetable bouillon	TO SERVE
		¼ cup unsalted butter	2 tbsp oil
serves 4		1 garlic clove, ground finely	2 oz/55 g mushrooms, sliced thinly
		2 cups assorted fresh and/or dried mushrooms (eg shiitake, portabellini, ceps, porcini) sliced	4 tsp flavored oil, to garnish
35 minutes + 30 minutes to soak mushrooms			
20 minutes			

If you are using dried mushrooms, soak them in boiling water for 30 minutes before you start cooking. Drain well and slice. Use the soaking liquid to replace an equal amount of bouillon.

Prepare the basic risotto as on page 8.

Add the extra butter, garlic, and 1½ cups of the mushrooms along with the onion at the very beginning of the process.

While the risotto is cooking, heat the extra oil in a small skillet. Add the last ½ cup of mushrooms and cook over a high heat until lightly browned and beginning to crisp. Remove from the heat and drain the mushrooms carefully.

Arrange the risotto on individual plates and sprinkle with the cooked mushrooms. Drizzle each portion with 1 teaspoon of flavored oil and serve.

mushroom
& white wine risotto

		ingredients
	very easy	1 quantity basic risotto (see page 8) made with white wine or half white wine and half bouillon
	serves 4	2 cups white mushrooms, sliced thinly
	10 minutes	2 cups eggplant, diced
		4 sprigs fresh thyme, to garnish
	20 minutes	

Prepare the basic risotto as on page 8, adding the mushrooms and eggplant along with the onion at the very beginning.

When the risotto is cooked, arrange on individual plates and garnish each one with a sprig of fresh thyme before serving.

asparagus & sun-dried
tomato risotto

very easy	**ingredients**

serves 4	1 quantity basic risotto (see page 8)
	  made with half vegetable bouillon
	  and half dry white wine
	6 sun-dried tomatoes, sliced thinly
	12 stalks fresh asparagus, cooked
	2 tsp lemon zest, grated finely

10 minutes	
20 minutes	

Prepare the basic risotto as on page 8, adding the tomatoes along with the onion at the very beginning.

While the risotto is cooking, cut 8 of the asparagus stalks into pieces about 2.5 cm/1 inch long. Keep 4 stalks whole for garnishing the finished dish.

Carefully fold the cut pieces of asparagus into the risotto for the last 5 minutes of cooking time.

Arrange the risotto on individual serving dishes and garnish with whole stalks of asparagus. Scatter lemon zest on top and serve.

blue cheese risotto

		ingredients
	very easy	1 quantity basic risotto (see page 8) made with vegetable bouillon
	serves 4	¼ cup vegetarian bacon strips, diced
		½ cup cup Dolcelatte or Gorgonzola, diced or crumbled
	5 minutes	salt and pepper
	20 minutes	

Prepare the basic risotto as on page 8, adding the vegetarian bacon along with the onion at the very beginning. Sauté until bacon is just starting to brown.

Stir half of the blue cheese into the risotto instead of the Parmesan in the basic risotto recipe and stir well to melt. Season well with lots of black pepper.

Arrange the risotto on individual plates. Crumble or dice the remaining blue cheese and sprinkle over the top of the risotto before serving.

four cheese risotto

		ingredients
	very easy	1 quantity basic risotto (see page 8) made with half vegetable bouillon and half dry white wine
	serves 4	½ cup Gorgonzola or Dolcelatte
		½ cup Fontina or Mozzarella
	5 minutes	½ cup Mascarpone
		salt and pepper
	20 minutes	

Prepare the basic risotto as on page 8.

Dice or grate the cheeses and keep some aside to garnish the risotto. Mix the rest into the risotto toward the end of the cooking time, along with the Parmesan in the basic risotto recipe. Stir well to melt.

Season well with lots of black pepper.

Arrange the risotto on individual plates. Scatter the remaining cheese over the top of the risotto before serving.

risotto with
artichoke hearts

		ingredients
extremely easy		1 quantity basic risotto (see page 8)
serves 4		8 oz/225 g canned artichoke hearts, drained and diced
10 minutes		
20 minutes		

Drain the artichoke hearts, reserving the liquid, and cut them into fourths.

Add the artichoke liquid to the bouillon being used for the risotto, but reduce the amount of your main liquid by the same amount as the liquid you are adding. Heat as for basic risotto on page 8.

Follow the procedure for basic risotto as on page 8, adding the artichoke hearts during the last 5 minutes of cooking time to heat them through. Serve immediately.

risotto with
roasted vegetables

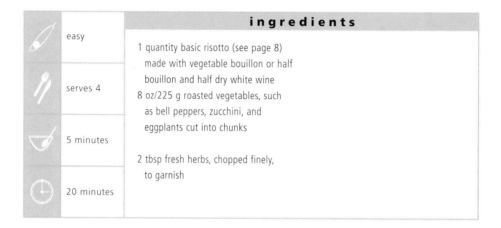

	ingredients
easy	1 quantity basic risotto (see page 8) made with vegetable bouillon or half bouillon and half dry white wine
serves 4	8 oz/225 g roasted vegetables, such as bell peppers, zucchini, and eggplants cut into chunks
5 minutes	2 tbsp fresh herbs, chopped finely, to garnish
20 minutes	

Prepare the basic risotto as on page 8, adding most of the roasted vegetables during the last 5 minutes of cooking time to heat them through. Set aside a few large pieces to use as a garnish.

Place the risotto on individual plates. Arrange vegetables around it or on top to garnish and then scatter with fresh herbs before serving immediately.

crispy vegetable risotto

		ingredients	
very easy		1 quantity basic risotto (see page 8) made with water or vegetable bouillon	2 oz/55 g snow peas, cut into $\frac{1}{2}$ inch/1 cm pieces
serves 4		3 tbsp butter 2 celery stalks, cut into $\frac{1}{2}$ inch/1 cm pieces	2 oz/55 g carrots, peeled and cut into $\frac{1}{2}$ inch/1 cm pieces 2 oz/55 g baby corn, blanched and cut into $\frac{1}{2}$ inch/1 cm pieces
10 minutes		2 oz/55 g green beans, cut into $\frac{1}{2}$ inch/1 cm pieces	
20 minutes			

Prepare the basic risotto as on page 8.

Meanwhile, melt the butter in a pan over a medium heat. Add all the vegetables, and stir to coat with butter, then cook for 5 minutes. They should remain crisp.

Carefully mix the vegetables into the risotto 5 minutes before the end of cooking time. Keep 2 tablespoons in reserve to be used as a garnish.

Arrange the risotto on individual plates and sprinkle with the reserved vegetables before serving.

green risotto
with leeks

		ingredients
	extremely easy	1 quantity basic risotto (see page 8) made with vegetable bouillon
	serves 4	4 oz/115 g leeks, washed and sliced thinly 8 oz/225 g fresh spinach, washed and sliced thinly
	10 minutes	oil for shallow frying 4 tbsp arugula, shredded (optional)
	20 minutes	

Prepare the basic risotto as on page 8, adding the leeks and spinach along with the onion at the very beginning. Reserve 2 tablespoons of the leeks to use for a garnish.

While the risotto is cooking, heat the oil in a skillet over a high heat. Add the reserved leeks and cook quickly until golden brown and crisp. Drain well and set aside.

If using arugula, stir it into the risotto during the last 5 minutes of cooking time.

Arrange the risotto on individual serving plates, scatter the cooked leeks on top of each portion to garnish, then serve immediately.

lentil & carrot risotto

		ingredients	
	extremely easy	1 quantity basic risotto (see page 8) made with vegetable bouillon	GARNISH 1 tbsp butter
	serves 4	1 cup cooked lentils ¾ cup carrots, grated	2 tbsp scallions, chopped finely
	5 minutes		
	20 minutes		

Prepare the basic risotto as on page 8, adding the lentils and carrots along with the onion at the very beginning.

While the risotto is cooking, melt the butter in a small skillet over a medium heat. Add the scallions and cook for 3–4 minutes to soften.

Serve the risotto on individual plates with scallions sprinkled on top to garnish.

double tomato risotto

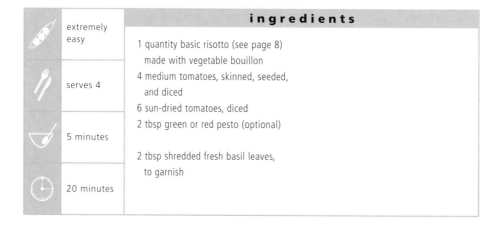

		ingredients
 	extremely easy	1 quantity basic risotto (see page 8) made with vegetable bouillon
	serves 4	4 medium tomatoes, skinned, seeded, and diced 6 sun-dried tomatoes, diced
	5 minutes	2 tbsp green or red pesto (optional) 2 tbsp shredded fresh basil leaves, to garnish
	20 minutes	

Prepare the basic risotto as on page 8, adding the fresh and sun-dried tomatoes along with the onion at the very beginning.

If using pesto, stir it into the risotto during the last 5 minutes of cooking time.

Serve the risotto garnished with shredded fresh basil leaves.

chile egg risotto

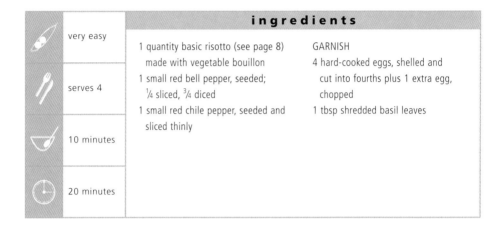

		ingredients	
very easy		1 quantity basic risotto (see page 8) made with vegetable bouillon	GARNISH 4 hard-cooked eggs, shelled and
serves 4		1 small red bell pepper, seeded; ¼ sliced, ¾ diced	cut into fourths plus 1 extra egg, chopped
10 minutes		1 small red chile pepper, seeded and sliced thinly	1 tbsp shredded basil leaves
20 minutes			

Prepare the basic risotto as on page 8, adding the diced red bell pepper and hot chile pepper along with the onion at the very beginning. Gently fold the eggs into the risotto during the last 5 minutes of cooking time.

Arrange the risotto on individual plates and sprinkle with the chopped egg, slices of bell pepper, and shredded basil and serve.

red wine, herb
& sun-dried tomato risotto

		ingredients
very easy		1 quantity basic risotto (see page 8)
		6 sun-dried tomatoes, chopped finely
serves 4		1 tbsp chopped fresh thyme
		1 tbsp chopped fresh parsley
5 minutes		10–12 basil leaves, shredded, to garnish
20 minutes		

Prepare the basic risotto as on page 8, using a mixture of half each strong Italian red wine and half vegetable bouillon, folding in the sun-dried tomatoes at the beginning of cooking.

Carefully fold the herbs into the risotto 5 minutes before the end of cooking time.

Serve the risotto garnished with the shredded fresh basil leaves.

herbs
& nuts

There is nothing quite like a handful of fresh herbs for adding taste, aroma, and a light, sophisticated touch to a hearty, filling risotto. So, whether you choose Lemon & Rosemary Risotto or Basic Basil Risotto or even Mint & Pea Risotto, you're guaranteed a delicious and satisfying meal. Nuts, on the other hand, can provide a deep, rich flavor and a delicious texture to the basic risotto recipe, particularly when mixed with Dolcelatte and Mascarpone, as in Crunchy Walnut Risotto.

herb risotto

		ingredients
extremely easy		1 quantity basic risotto (see page 8) made with chicken or vegetable bouillon
serves 4		1 zucchini, peeled and diced large handful mixed herbs, chopped finely
10 minutes		
20 minutes		

Prepare the basic risotto as on page 8, adding the zucchini along with the onion at the very beginning.

Carefully fold most of the herbs into the risotto 5 minutes before the end of cooking time.

Serve the risotto on individual plates and sprinkle each with a generous amount of herbs to garnish.

lemon & rosemary risotto

		ingredients

	extremely easy	2 lemons
		1 quantity basic risotto (see page 8)
		  made with vegetable
		  or chicken bouillon
		1 tbsp fresh rosemary, chopped finely

	serves 4	
	10 minutes	
	20 minutes	

Grate the lemon zest and set aside.

Squeeze the juice from the lemons into a small pan and place over a medium heat until just about to boil. Use the lemon juice to replace an equal amount of bouillon when preparing the basic risotto on page 8.

Add half of the rosemary to the onions when you begin preparing the risotto. Gently stir the remainder in when the risotto has finished cooking.

Arrange the risotto on individual plates and sprinkle with lemon zest before serving.

mint & pea risotto

		ingredients
	extremely easy	1 quantity basic risotto (see page 8) made with chicken bouillon
	serves 4	1 cup frozen peas 4 tbsp fresh mint leaves, shredded
	5 minutes	
	20 minutes	

Prepare the basic risotto as on page 8, adding the peas along with the onion at the very beginning.

Stir most of the mint into the risotto for the last 5 minutes of cooking time.

Arrange the risotto on individual plates and sprinkle with the remaining mint before serving.

crunchy walnut risotto

		ingredients
very easy		1 quantity basic risotto (see page 8) made with chicken or vegetable bouillon
serves 4		2 tbsp butter
		1 cup walnut halves
5 minutes		½ cup Mascarpone, diced
		½ cup Dolcelatte, diced
20 minutes		

Prepare the basic risotto as on page 8, adding the Mascarpone and Dolcelatte at the same time as the Parmesan.

While the risotto is cooking, melt the butter in a skillet over a medium heat. Add the walnuts and toss for 2–3 minutes, or until just starting to brown. Stir most of the walnuts into the finished risotto and scatter the rest on top of each portion before serving.

fennel risotto

		ingredients
extremely easy		1 large fennel bulb
serves 4		1 quantity basic risotto (see page 8) made with either chicken bouillon or half bouillon and half dry white wine
10 minutes		salt and pepper grated Parmesan, to garnish
20 minutes		

Trim the fennel and slice in half, then slice thinly. Prepare the basic risotto as on page 8, adding the fennel along with the onion at the very beginning.

Sprinkle with lots of black pepper and grated Parmesan and serve immediately.

basic basil risotto

		ingredients
	very easy	1 quantity basic risotto (see page 8)
		10–12 fresh basil leaves
	serves 4	4 fresh tomatoes, seeded and diced
		4 oz/115 g green beans, cooked
	10 minutes	2 tbsp pine nuts, to garnish
	20 minutes	

Prepare the basic risotto as on page 8, adding half of the basil leaves (shredded), the tomatoes, and beans along with the onion at the very beginning. Cook gently for 2–3 minutes for the flavors to blend before adding the rice.

While the risotto is cooking, heat a skillet over a high heat. Add the pine nuts and dry-fry for 1–2 minutes, or until just starting to brown. Be careful not to let them burn.

When the risotto is cooked, tear and carefully fold in half of the remaining fresh basil.

Use the last of the basil leaves, whole, to garnish each serving and sprinkle with pine nuts before serving.

fish
& seafood

Take two favorite ingredients—the freshest fish or seafood you can find and succulent risotto—put them together to create infinite combinations for some of the simplest and most delicious dishes imaginable. Herbs, tomatoes, wine, and cheese complement fish and seafood beautifully. When they are mixed with a well cooked risotto, you are in for a treat.

seafood risotto

		ingredients	
easy		1 quantity basic risotto (see page 8) made with dry white wine or vegetable bouillon	2 garlic cloves, sliced thinly $\frac{1}{4}$ cup dry white wine
serves 4		1 lb/450 g mussels or clams $\frac{1}{4}$ cup unsalted butter 1 shallot, sliced thinly	2 tbsp chopped fresh parsley, to garnish
10 minutes			
20 minutes			

Prepare basic risotto as on on page 8. While the risotto is cooking, prepare the mussels or clams by scrubbing well to remove any barnacles or "beards." If any of the shells are open, tap sharply on the work surface. If they do not close, discard.

Melt the butter in a heavy-based pan. Add the shallot and garlic and cook for 3 minutes to soften. Add the mussels and wine, then put a lid on the pan and cook over a high heat for 10 minutes, shaking the pan occasionally, until all the shells have opened.

Remove the mussels from the pan, draining well. Do not discard the shallots or pan juices. Remove some of the mussels from their shells, but leave some as they are. If any have not opened, discard. Gently fold the shelled mussels into the risotto. Spoon onto plates and garnish with the mussels that are still in their shells. Boil the shallot and wine mixture; reduce until thickened, then remove from the heat and pour over each portion. Sprinkle with parsley and serve.

risotto marinara

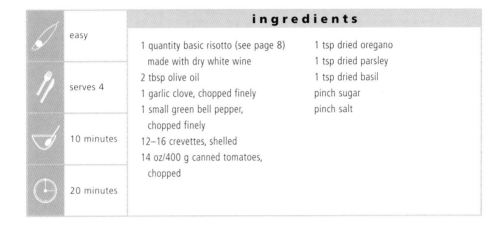

		ingredients	
easy		1 quantity basic risotto (see page 8) made with dry white wine	1 tsp dried oregano
			1 tsp dried parsley
serves 4		2 tbsp olive oil	1 tsp dried basil
		1 garlic clove, chopped finely	pinch sugar
		1 small green bell pepper, chopped finely	pinch salt
10 minutes		12–16 crevettes, shelled	
		14 oz/400 g canned tomatoes, chopped	
20 minutes			

Prepare the basic risotto according to the instructions on page 8. While the risotto is cooking, heat the oil in a large, heavy-based skillet. Toss in the garlic and bell pepper and cook over a high heat for 2 minutes.

Add the crevettes and cook until pink all over, stirring frequently.

Add the tomatoes and flavorings. Once the tomatoes have come to a boil, reduce the heat and cover the skillet, then cook for an additional 5 minutes.

Carefully remove the crevettes from the sauce.

Place the risotto on serving plates and arrange the crevettes on top. Spoon some of the tomato sauce over each portion and pass the rest separately. Serve immediately.

risotto with tuna
& pine nuts

		ingredients	
very easy	1 quantity basic risotto (see page 8) made with dry white wine or vegetable bouillon	1 tsp fresh marjoram, chopped finely
serves 4	8 oz/225 g tuna fish (canned or broiled fresh steaks)	2 tbsp white wine vinegar / salt and pepper / ⅓ cup olive oil / ⅓ cup pine nuts
10 minutes	8–10 black olives, pitted and sliced / 1 small pimiento, sliced thinly / 1 tsp fresh parsley, chopped finely	1 garlic clove, chopped / 8 oz/225 g fresh tomatoes, skinned, deseeded, and diced
20 minutes		

Prepare the risotto according to the instructions on page 8.

While the risotto is cooking, flake the tuna and mix in a large bowl with the olives, pimiento, parsley, marjoram, and vinegar. Season to taste with salt and pepper.

Heat the olive oil in a small skillet over a high heat. Add the pine nuts and garlic. Sauté gently for 2 minutes, or until they just begin to brown.

Add the tomatoes to the skillet and mix well. Continue cooking over a medium heat for 3–4 minutes, or until they are thoroughly warm.

Pour the tomatoes over the tuna and mix. Fold into the risotto 5 minutes before the end of cooking time. Serve immediately.

risotto with squid
& garlic butter

		ingredients
	very easy	8–12 baby squid
		1 quantity basic risotto (see page 8)
		made with dry white wine or
	serves 4	vegetable bouillon
		½ cup unsalted butter
		3 garlic cloves, crushed
	10 minutes	
		2 tbsp fresh parsley, chopped finely,
		to garnish
	25 minutes	

Clean the squid, carefully removing and discarding the innards and the membrane lining it. Dice the tentacles. Score the squid with a sharp knife, making both horizontal and vertical cuts.

Prepare the basic risotto according to the instructions on page 8.

Melt the butter in a heavy-based skillet. Add the garlic and cook over a low heat for 2 minutes, or until soft.

Increase the heat to high, then add the squid and toss to cook. This should take no more than 2–3 minutes or the squid will get tough. Remove the squid from the skillet, draining carefully and reserving the garlic butter.

Place the risotto on serving plates and arrange the squid on top. Spoon some of the garlic butter over each portion. Sprinkle with parsley and serve immediately.

risotto with sole
& tomatoes

		ingredients	
	very easy	1 quantity basic risotto (see page 8) made with red wine	$\frac{1}{4}$ cup red wine
	serves 4	2 tbsp olive oil	1 lb/450 g sole or flounder fillets, skinned
		1 lb/450 g fresh tomatoes, skinned, deseeded, and cut into strips	
	10 minutes	6 sun-dried tomatoes, sliced thinly	2 tbsp fresh cilantro, chopped finely, to garnish
		3 tbsp tomato paste	
	20 minutes		

Prepare the basic risotto according to the instructions on page 8.

While the risotto is cooking, heat the oil in a large, heavy-based skillet. Add the fresh and dried tomatoes. Stir well and cook over a medium heat for 10–15 minutes, or until soft and slushy.

Stir in the tomato paste and red wine. Bring the sauce to a boil, then reduce the heat until it is just simmering.

Cut the fish into strips and add to the sauce. Stir gently. Cook for 5 minutes, or until the fish flakes when checked with a fork. Most of the liquid should be absorbed, but if it isn't, remove the fish and then increase the heat to reduce the sauce.

Place the risotto on serving plates and arrange the fish and sauce on top. Garnish with fresh cilantro and serve immediately.

lobster or monkfish risotto

		ingredients
easy		1 quantity basic risotto (see page 8) made with dry white wine or vegetable bouillon
serves 4		¼ cup butter
		1 lb/450 g lobster meat, shelled langoustines, or monkfish, cooked
5 minutes		2 tbsp brandy
20 minutes		1 tbsp finely grated orange zest, to garnish

Prepare the basic risotto according to the instructions on page 8.

While the risotto is cooking, melt the butter in a large, heavy-based skillet.

Cut the lobster (or monkfish, if using) into large chunks, then add to the butter and toss well to coat. Cook for 3–4 minutes over a medium heat.

Warm the brandy in a ladle over a high flame, then pour over the lobster and set alight. Shake the pan to coat the lobster in sauce.

Carefully fold the lobster into the risotto for its last 5 minutes of cooking. Serve on individual plates garnished with orange zest.

meat
& poultry

Risotto is particularly filling and generally served as a main course with garnishes or flavorings. When serving with meat and poultry, you can cook up a storm with unusual spicy sausages for Sausage & Bell Pepper Risotto or create the delicious barbecue-style dish of Risotto with Chargrilled Chicken Breast. If using meat or poultry, be careful not to let it overwhelm the focus of the dish and make the rest of the meal very light to achieve a balance.

shredded spinach
& ham risotto

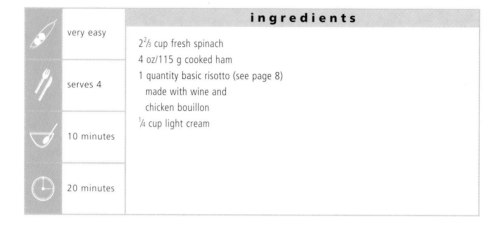

		ingredients
	very easy	2²/₃ cup fresh spinach
		4 oz/115 g cooked ham
	serves 4	1 quantity basic risotto (see page 8)
		made with wine and
		chicken bouillon
	10 minutes	¼ cup light cream
	20 minutes	

Wash the spinach well and slice into thin shreds.

Cut the ham into thin strips.

Prepare basic risotto as on page 8. Add the spinach and ham when you add the last ladleful of bouillon. Mix well.

Add the cream to the risotto when stirring in the last knob of butter and Parmesan cheese. Serve immediately.

sausage & bell pepper risotto

		ingredients	
	very easy	8 sausages, sweet and/or spicy	2 tbsp olive oil
		1 red bell pepper, seeded and	1 quantity basic risotto (see page 8)
	serves 4	cut into 8 pieces	made with meat bouillon or bouillon
		1 green bell pepper, seeded and	and red wine
		cut into 8 pieces	
	10 minutes	1 medium onion, sliced thickly	rosemary sprigs, to garnish
	20–30 minutes		

Preheat the oven to 375°F/190°C.

Place the sausages in a large, shallow ovenproof dish.

Scatter the bell pepper and onion around the sausages. Sprinkle with olive oil.

Cook the sausages and vegetables in the oven for 20–30 minutes, turning occasionally.

Prepare the basic risotto as on page 8.

Arrange a large scoop of risotto on each plate and sprinkle with bell peppers and onions. Place two sausages per person on either side of the risotto, then garnish with rosemary sprigs and serve immediately.

risotto with chargrilled chicken breast

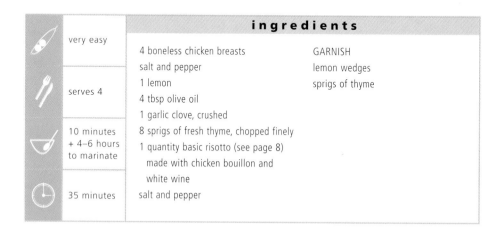

		ingredients	
very easy	4 boneless chicken breasts		GARNISH
	salt and pepper		lemon wedges
	1 lemon		sprigs of thyme
serves 4	4 tbsp olive oil		
	1 garlic clove, crushed		
10 minutes + 4–6 hours to marinate	8 sprigs of fresh thyme, chopped finely		
	1 quantity basic risotto (see page 8) made with chicken bouillon and white wine		
35 minutes	salt and pepper		

Arrange the chicken breasts in a shallow dish. Season to taste. Grate the lemon zest into a mixing bowl. Add the juice of the lemon, olive oil, garlic, and thyme. Mix, then spoon over the chicken and rub in. Cover with plastic wrap and put in the refrigerator to marinate for 4–6 hours.

Remove the chicken from the refrigerator so that it returns to room temperature. Preheat a griddle over a high heat. Put the chicken, skin side down, on the griddle and cook for 10 minutes, or until the skin is crisp and starting to brown. Turn over and brown the underside. Reduce the heat and cook for 10–15 minutes more, or until the juices run clear when pierced with a skewer.

Prepare the basic risotto as on page 8. Transfer the chicken to a carving board. Let rest for 5 minutes, then cut into thick slices. Put a scoop of risotto on each plate and arrange the chicken slices. Garnish with lemon wedges and thyme and serve.

risotto croquettes

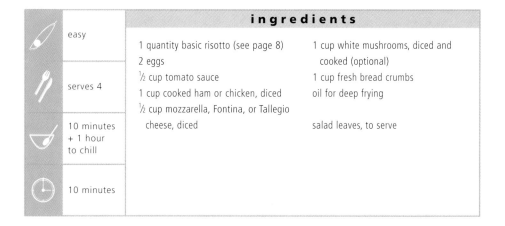

		ingredients	
easy		1 quantity basic risotto (see page 8)	1 cup white mushrooms, diced and
		2 eggs	cooked (optional)
serves 4		½ cup tomato sauce	1 cup fresh bread crumbs
		1 cup cooked ham or chicken, diced	oil for deep frying
		½ cup mozzarella, Fontina, or Tallegio	
10 minutes + 1 hour to chill		cheese, diced	salad leaves, to serve
10 minutes			

Let the risotto cool completely, then mix with 1 beaten egg, the tomato sauce, ham, cheese, and mushrooms (if using). The tomato sauce can be spicy, if you prefer.

Form spoonfuls of the mixture into patties or ovals and place on a large plate. Cover the plate with plastic wrap and chill for 1 hour.

Heat the oil in a wok or deep skillet.

Remove the croquettes from the refrigerator. Beat the second egg in a small bowl and dip the croquettes in it. Drain and coat in bread crumbs. Shake off any excess crumbs and gently drop the croquettes into the hot oil. Cook for 5 minutes until thoroughly heated and golden brown. Remove carefully, and drain on paper towels, then cool for a few minutes before serving either at room temperature or cold.

spicy pork risotto

		ingredients	
very easy		1 thick slice crustless white bread	14 oz /400 g canned tomatoes,
		water or milk, to soak	chopped
serves 4		4 cups ground pork	1 tbsp tomato paste
		2 garlic cloves, chopped finely	1 tsp dried oregano
		1 tbsp finely ground onion	1 tsp fennel seeds
10 minutes		1 tsp black peppercorns, crushed	pinch of sugar
		pinch of salt	1 quantity basic risotto (see page 8)
		1 egg	made with meat bouillon and
45 minutes		oil for browning	red wine
			basil leaves, to garnish

Soak the bread in the water or milk for 5 minutes to soften. Drain and squeeze to remove all the liquid. Mix the bread, pork, garlic, onion, peppercorns, and salt in a bowl. Add the egg and mix well.

Heat the oil in a skillet over a medium heat. Form the meat mixture into balls and brown a few at a time in the oil. Remove from the pan and then drain, set aside until all the balls are cooked.

Combine the tomatoes, tomato paste, herbs, and sugar in a heavy-based skillet. Add the meatballs. Bring the sauce to a boil over a medium heat, then reduce and simmer for 45 minutes, or until the meat is thoroughly cooked.

Prepare the basic risotto as on page 8. When the meatballs are cooked, lift out and add to the risotto. Mix carefully, but avoid breaking up the mixture. Arrange the risotto and a few meatballs on plates. Drizzle with tomato sauce, then garnish with basil and serve.

hot bell pepper lamb
in red wine risotto

		ingredients	
very easy		4 tbsp all–purpose flour	2 garlic cloves, sliced thinly
		salt and pepper	2 tbsp fresh basil, torn coarsely
serves 4		$\frac{1}{4}$ cup olive oil	$\frac{1}{2}$ cup red wine
		8 pieces neck of lamb or lamb chops	4 tbsp red wine vinegar
		1 green bell pepper, seeded and	8 cherry tomatoes
		sliced thinly	$\frac{1}{2}$ cup water
20 minutes		1 or 2 fresh green chile peppers,	1 quantity basic risotto (see page 8)
		seeded and sliced thinly	made with beef bouillon and
		1 small onion, sliced thinly	red wine
30 minutes			

Mix the flour with salt and pepper on a plate. Heat the oil over a high heat in a skillet large enough to take all the lamb in a single layer. Dredge the lamb in the flour, shaking off any excess. Put the lamb in the skillet and brown. Remove and set aside.

Toss the green bell pepper, chile pepper(s), onion, garlic, and basil in the oil left in the skillet then cook for 3 minutes, or until lightly browned. Add the wine and vinegar, then bring to a boil and continue cooking over a high heat for 3–4 minutes, or until reduced to 2 tablespoons.

Add the tomatoes and water to the casserole, then stir and bring to a boil. Return the meat, then cover and reduce the heat as low as possible. Cook for 30 minutes, or until the meat is tender, turning occasionally. Check regularly and add 2–3 tablespoons of water if necessary. Prepare the basic risotto as on page 8. Arrange a scoop of risotto on each plate and sprinkle with the peppers and tomatoes. Arrange the lamb and serve.

chef's specials

Although the risotto for these recipes
follows the basic method, it is the way in
which it is used, or the accompaniments,
that elevate it into the "specials" category.
Most of the techniques are easy, but some
of the ingredients may be a little bit more
extravagant and challenging to track down.
Definitely not your everyday recipes, Fried
Rice Cakes, Lemon & Veal Risotto, and
Risotto Milanese are among those recipes
you can use to celebrate special occasions.

fried rice cakes

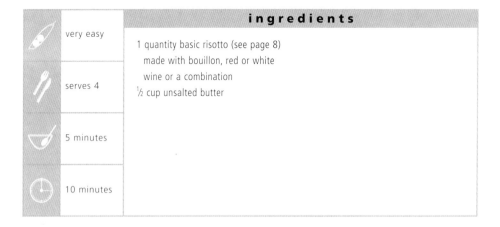

		ingredients
very easy		1 quantity basic risotto (see page 8) made with bouillon, red or white wine or a combination
serves 4		½ cup unsalted butter
5 minutes		
10 minutes		

If you are making the risotto specially for this recipe, let it cool thoroughly. Otherwise, use leftover risotto, which is better used this way than reheated in a pan or microwave.

Melt 2 tablespoons of butter over a medium heat in a heavy skillet until it is foaming. Form 1 heaped tablespoon of risotto into a thin cake. Gently place in the butter and cook until thoroughly heated and golden on both sides—about 5 minutes. Remove from the skillet and keep warm while you repeat the process and use up all the risotto.

stuffed rice balls

		ingredients	
very easy		1 quantity basic risotto (see page 8) made with bouillon, red or white wine, or a combination	4 tbsp cooked ham, cubed (optional) 4 tbsp spicy tomato sauce (optional) 1 egg, beaten
serves 4		½ cup mozzarella, Fontina, or Taleggio cheese, cubed (optional)	2 cups fresh bread crumbs oil for deep-frying
10 minutes + 20 minutes to chill			
10 minutes			

If you are making the risotto specially for this recipe, let it cool thoroughly. Otherwise, use leftover risotto which is better used this way than reheated in a pan or microwave.

Place 1 heaped tablespoon of risotto in the palm of your hand and flatten slightly. Top with a cube of cheese or ham or a teaspoon of tomato sauce (if using). Place another tablespoon of risotto on top and close gently to form a ball. Make sure the filling is completely enclosed or it will leak when cooking. Arrange the rice balls on a plate and chill for 10 minutes.

Remove the rice balls from the refrigerator. Dip in beaten egg and then roll in bread crumbs, shaking off any excess. Chill for another 10 minutes before cooking. Heat the oil in a wok or deep skillet. Gently lower the rice balls into the hot oil and cook until thoroughly heated and golden brown. Remove carefully and drain on paper towels. Let cool slightly but serve warm.

pumpkin chestnut risotto

		ingredients	
very easy		1 quantity basic risotto (see page 8) made with white wine and chicken bouillon 8 oz/225 g pumpkin, diced	8 oz/225 g chestnuts, cooked and shelled 1 tsp saffron threads, optional
serves 4			
10 minutes			
20 minutes			

Prepare the basic risotto as on page 8, adding the pumpkin at the same time as the onion. Cook gently until starting to color.

Coarsely chop the chestnuts and add to the rice and pumpkin mixture. Stir thoroughly to coat.

If using saffron, dissolve it in 4 tablespoons of hot bouillon and add to the rice after the wine has been absorbed. Serve immediately.

saffron & lemon risotto
with scallops

		ingredients	
extremely easy		1 quantity basic risotto (see page 8) made with fish or chicken bouillon 1 tsp saffron threads 16 scallops 2 tbsp vegetable oil juice of 1 lemon	GARNISH 1 lemon, cut into wedges 2 tsp grated lemon zest
serves 4			
5 minutes + 15 minutes to chill			
25 minutes			

Place the scallops in a bowl and mix with the lemon juice. Cover the bowl with plastic wrap and refrigerate for 15 minutes.

Meanwhile, prepare the basic risotto as on page 8.

Dissolve the saffron in 4 tablespoons of hot bouillon and add to the rice with the first ladleful of liquid.

When the risotto is nearly cooked, preheat a griddle over a high heat. Brush the scallops with oil and sear on the griddle for 3–4 minutes on each side, depending on their thickness. Take care not to overcook or they will be rubbery.

Season the risotto with lemon juice, adding just 1 teaspoon at a time and tasting as you go.

Place a large scoop of risotto on each plate. Arrange 4 scallops and lemon wedges around it, then sprinkle with grated lemon zest and serve immediately.

lemon & veal risotto

		ingredients
easy		
	2 tbsp olive oil	¼ cup water
	1 lb/450 g veal cutlets, beaten thin	1 quantity basic risotto (see page 8)
serves 4	1 tsp dried oregano	made with chicken bouillon or
	1 tsp dried thyme	bouillon and white wine
	salt and pepper	
	2 tbsp lemon juice	2 tsp lemon zest, grated finely,
5 minutes	¼ cup dry white wine	to garnish
25 minutes		

Prepare the basic risotto as on page 8.

Sprinkle the olive oil over the veal. Rub in the herbs, salt, and pepper.

Heat a non-stick skillet and brown the veal quickly over a high heat, turning once.

Pour over the lemon juice, wine, and water. Bring to a boil, then reduce the heat. Cover and simmer gently for 15 minutes.

When the meat is cooked through, transfer to a serving dish and garnish with lemon zest. Serve the risotto on the side.

risotto with radicchio
& mozzarella

		ingredients
	very easy	1 quantity basic risotto (see page 8) made with chicken bouillon or water
	serves 4	1 large head radicchio, sliced thinly 1 cup mozzarella or provolone, diced
	5 minutes	
	20 minutes	

Prepare the basic risotto according to the recipe on page 8.
Add the radicchio to the rice about 5 minutes before the end of
the cooking time. It should have just enough time to soften
slightly and absorb some of the flavor.

Omit the Parmesan from the recipe, but add the mozzarella
(or provolone, if using) to the cooked risotto. Stir until it melts
and serve immediately.

scallion risotto
with grilled lime

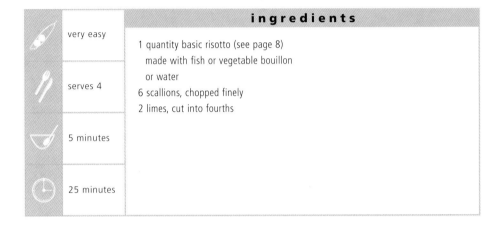

		ingredients
very easy		1 quantity basic risotto (see page 8) made with fish or vegetable bouillon or water
serves 4		6 scallions, chopped finely
5 minutes		2 limes, cut into fourths
25 minutes		

Prepare the basic risotto as on page 8, substituting scallions for onion.

While the risotto is cooking, cook the limes on a griddle preheated over a high heat. Turn frequently until they are brown all over and the juices are sizzling.

Arrange the limes around the risotto and serve immediately.

risotto milanese

		ingredients
extremely easy		1 tsp saffron threads
serves 4		1 quantity basic risotto (see page 8) made with half chicken bouillon and half dry white wine
5 minutes		
20 minutes		

Heat the bouillon for the risotto according to the recipe on page 8.

Infuse the saffron threads in the bouillon. Continue simmering for 5 minutes before beginning to add to the rice.

Prepare the basic risotto as on page 8 and serve immediately.

index